My Millennium Record Book

DK Publishing, Inc.

Personal Profile

My Horoscope

Zodiac star sign..................

Five words that describe my character are:

1..
2..
3..
4..
5..

Chinese horoscope animal

....

Top Secrets

Greatest love..............................

Biggest fear..............................

Pet peeves..............................

Best kept secret..............................

Secret password..............................

Millennium Me

A photograph of me.

My name.............................

Nickname.............................

Birthday.............................

Exact age on January 1, 2000:

.......years......months......days

My private fact file and record of my top secrets,

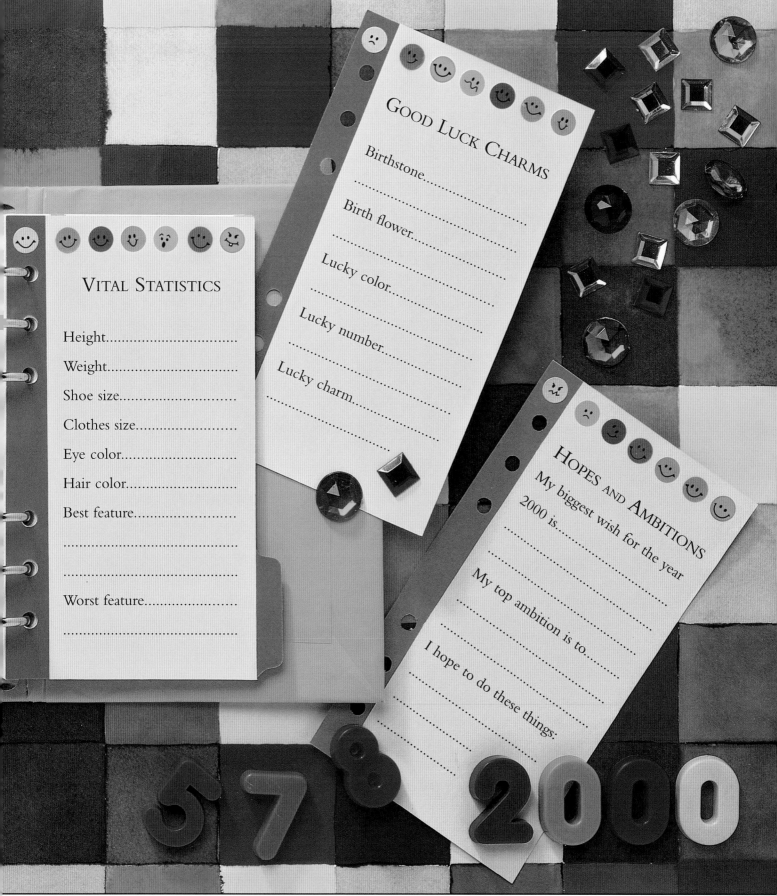

GOOD LUCK CHARMS

Birthstone...................................
....

Birth flower..............................
....

Lucky color...............................
....

Lucky number............................
....

Lucky charm..............................
....

VITAL STATISTICS

Height....................................

Weight....................................

Shoe size.................................

Clothes size..............................

Eye color.................................

Hair color................................

Best feature..............................
....
....

Worst feature............................
....

HOPES AND AMBITIONS

My biggest wish for the year
2000 is..............................
....
....

My top ambition is to............
....
....

I hope to do these things:
....
....

hopes, and ambitions for the new millennium.

Favorite Things

Favorite hobby

....

Best collection

....

Best toy

....

Favorite game

....

Favorite color

....

Favorite clothes

....

Best millennium souvenir

....

Most treasured object

....

My year 2000 collection of favorite sports,

Best place to eat

....

Favorite meal

....

Favorite sports team

....

Best sports star

....

Best vacation

....

Favorite season

....

Favorite animal

....

Best pet

....

hobbies, games, and treasures.

Pick of the Year

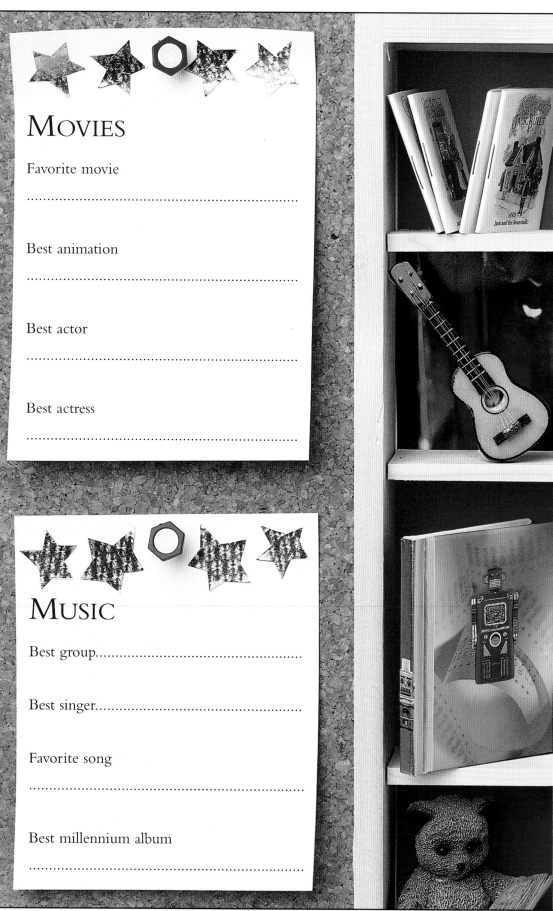

MOVIES

Favorite movie

....

Best animation

....

Best actor

....

Best actress

....

MUSIC

Best group...

Best singer..

Favorite song

....

Best millennium album

....

My millennium list of best books, great films, top

BOOKS

Favorite novel..

Best millennium book

....

Favorite author......................................

Best magazine..

TV PROGRAMS

Favorite program

....

Best TV star...

Favorite soap...

Best cartoon..

Best millennium program

....

tunes, and terrific TV.

Family

Fill the frames with family photographs.

My family portrait gallery and favorite photos of

relatives, pets, and our millennium celebrations.

Family Timeline

| January | February | March |
| July | August | September |

My year 2000 record of family birthdays, weddings,

April　　　May　　　June

October　　　November　✦　December

anniversaries, holidays, and other special days.

Home

MILLENNIUM BUG ATTACK!

Things that went haywire at home are.....

....

....

....

....

The worst thing that happened was.......

....

....

....

My drawing of the millennium bug

A PICTURE OF MY HOME

My family has lived here since...........

Home address

....

....

....

Telephone number

....

Email address

....

....

Millennium bug madness, my home address, and my

MY COLLECTION OF NEW MILLENNIUM POSTAGE STAMPS

FIRST MESSAGES
OF THE YEAR 2000

FIRST EMAIL

From..

Message..

....

....

FIRST PHONE CALL

Caller's name..

Message..

....

....

FIRST LETTER DELIVERY

From..

Message..

....

....

FIRST VISITOR 2000

Visitor's name..

Reason for visit......................................

....

My first letter and envelope go here.

first communications in the year 2000.

Class

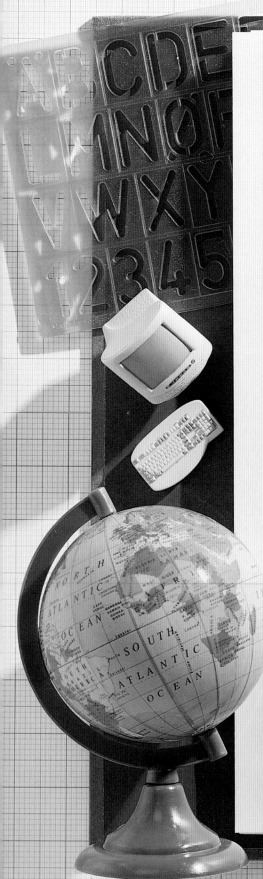

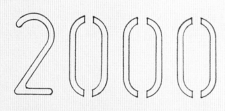

SCHOOL DETAILS

School name.........................

Address.............................

....

Telephone number

....

Principal............................

CLASS DETAILS

Homeroom number.............

Teacher...............................

Number of students.............

Favorite teacher..................

Worst teacher.....................

First day of school in the

year 2000.........................

WEEKLY TIMETABLE

DAY	a.m.	p.m.
Monday		
Tuesday		
Wednesday		
Thursday		
Friday		

SCHOOL REPORT

Best grades................. ....

Favorite subjects................................

Worst subjects................................

My school report, favorite teacher, best and worst

MILLENNIUM DIARY

My best memory of my school millennium celebration is.............................

....

....

....

....

....

....

SCHOOL TRIPS AND CLASS ACTIVITIES

Event	Rank out of 10
1..	☐
2..	☐
3..	☐
4..	☐
5..	☐

subjects, and year 2000 class celebrations.

Friends

BEST FRIEND
FACT FILE

A photograph goes here.

Name.................................

Nickname............................

Age....... Birthday................

Address..............................

....

Telephone number

....

Email address

....

Best feature............................

....

Worst feature..........................

....

Special talents.........................

....

Things we do together

....

....

Signature.............................

Things to do with friends in the new millennium

1.................................

....

2.................................

....

3.................................

....

My best friend, millennium pals, and going places

FRIEND FACT FILE

A photograph goes here.

Name......................

Nickname......................

Address......................

....

Telephone number

....

FRIEND FACT FILE

A photograph goes here.

Name......................

Nickname......................

Address......................

Telephone number

....

Signature......................

FRIEND FACT FILE

A photograph goes here.

Name......................

Nickname......................

Address......................

....

Telephone number

....

Signature......................

with friends this year.

Millennium Messages

Millennium Pals
forever! ☺☺

A collection of autographs and millennium

Keep Smiling ☺

messages from my friends, family, and favorite people.

New Millennium Day

HAPPY NEW YEAR!

I WILL ALWAYS REMEMBER TODAY BECAUSE..........

....

....

MY NEW YEAR'S RESOLUTIONS 2000

1..

2..

3..

4..

5..

My top five resolutions for the new millennium

HEADLINE NEWS

The big story of January 1, 2000 was...........................

....

TV headlines...

....

Newspaper headlines..

....

Best news..

....

Worst news..

....

and the headline news on January 1, 2000.

Millennium Trip

MILLENNIUM TRIP LOG

EVENT.....................................

PLACE.....................................

DATE.......................................

TIME OF ARRIVAL.....................

TIME OF DEPARTURE..................

PEOPLE ON THE TRIP.................
....

HOW WE TRAVELED....................
....

A photograph
of my visit
goes here.

My entry
ticket
goes here.

My favorite millennium event, where it was held,

Space for more photographs.

My favorite exhibits were..
....
....
....

I thought this trip was great because...........................
....
....
....
....
....

who went, and what was there.

Millennium Predictions

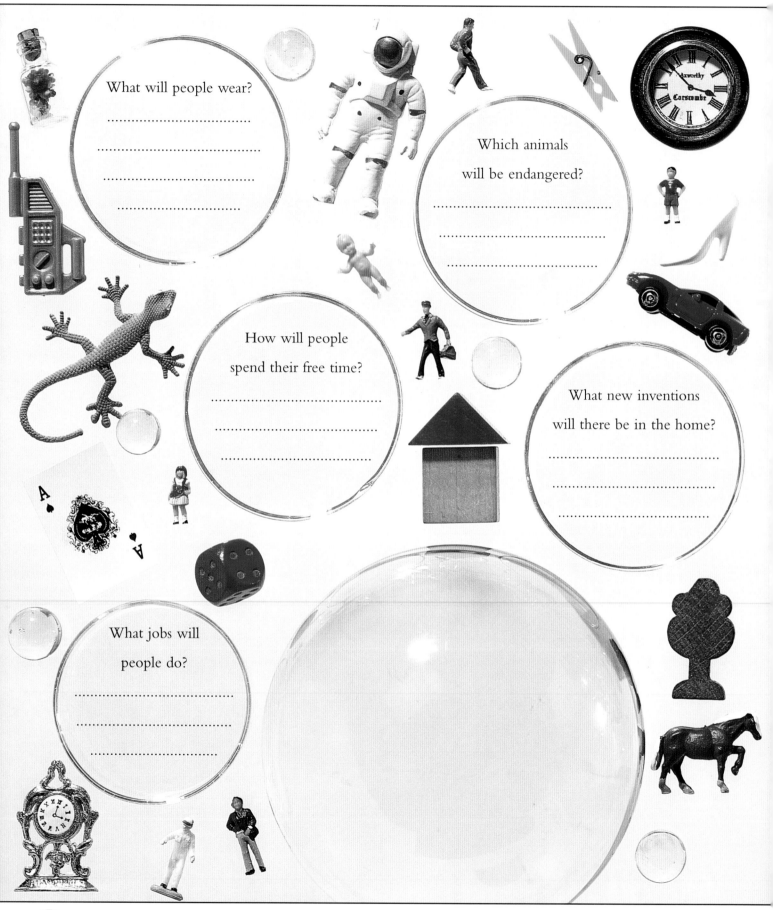

What will people wear?

....

....

....

....

Which animals
will be endangered?

....

....

....

How will people
spend their free time?

....

....

....

What new inventions
will there be in the home?

....

....

....

What jobs will
people do?

....

....

....

My top 10 predictions for the future and how our

Will new medicines stop people from getting ill?

....

....

What foods will people eat?

....

....

....

Will we find life in outer space?

....

....

....

How will our environment change?

....

....

....

MY CAR DESIGN OF THE FUTURE

How will people travel?

....

....

....

world will change in the new millennium.

Time Capsule

Dear friends of the future!

My present to you contains lots of things that tell you about my life in the year 2000.

....

....

....

....

....

....

....

....

....

....

....

....

Signed..................................

Date......................................

My gift to the children of the year 3000: a time

capsule of everyday objects and treasures.

Millennium Celebrations

January

- New Year's Day celebrations around the world
- The Millennium Dome opens in Greenwich, London

April

- The Pope delivers his Easter message in Rome, Italy

My diary of millennium events, celebrations,

February

- FEBRUARY 14TH: St. Valentine's Day
- CHINESE NEW YEAR: The Year of the Dragon

March

- CARNIVAL TIME in Rio de Janeiro, Brazil

May

- MAY 1ST: May Day celebrations around the world

June

- JUNE 21ST: Longest day of the year in the northern hemisphere and longest night in the southern hemisphere

IUBILAEUM

CHRISTUS HERI

HODIE SEMPER

A.D. 2000

festivals, and exhibitions around the world.

Millennium Celebrations

July

• THE SUMMER THEATER FESTIVAL begins in Avignon, France

August

• PLANET EARTH 2000: The International Garden Festival opens at Mount Penang, Australia

October

• OCTOBER 31ST: Halloween festivities

November

• NOVEMBER 23RD: Thanksgiving celebrations are held in the US

More diary notes of millennium events, festivals,

September

- THE 2000 OLYMPIC GAMES are held in Sydney, Australia

December

- FIRST CHRISTMAS of the new millennium

celebrations, and exhibitions around the world.

Millennium means 1,000 years!

It comes from the Latin words *mille* meaning one thousand and *annus* meaning year.

The year 2000 is a bimillennium!

In the Christian world, it marks the two thousandth anniversary of Christ's birth.

2001 – the real new millennium?

Some people think that January 1, 2001 is the true start to the new millennium.

The world's most popular calendar!

The year 2000 is part of the widely used Gregorian calendar, which was introduced in 1582 by Pope Gregory XIII. This Christian calendar normally has 365 days a year, as it's based on the time it takes the Earth to circle the Sun – 365.25 days.

The year 2000 is a leap year!

Every four years we add an extra day to our calendar on February 29. This makes up the extra 0.25 days that it takes the Earth to circle the Sun each year.

The world's biggest party!

Around two billion people will be celebrating the new millennium and its arrival on New Year's Eve, December 31, 1999.

Not all of the world is celebrating!

Two-thirds of the world's population is non-Christian and uses other calendars. The year 2000 is:

Year 4636 in the Chinese calendar.

Year 1420 in the Islamic calendar.

Year 5760 in the Jewish calendar.

A DK Publishing Book

www.dk.com

EDITOR • Jane Yorke
DESIGN • Jane Bull
MANAGING EDITOR • Mary Ling
MANAGING ART EDITOR • Rachael Foster
DTP DESIGNER • Almudena Díaz
PRODUCTION • Josie Alabaster
PHOTOGRAPHY BY • Andy Crawford
JACKET DESIGN • Andrew Nash

First American Edition, 1999

2 4 6 8 10 9 7 5 3

Published in the United States by
DK Publishing, Inc.
95 Madison Avenue
New York, New York 10016

Copyright © 1999 Dorling Kindersley
Limited

ISBN: 0-7894-4713-4

Color reproduction by
Colourscan, Singapore
Printed and bound in China by
L. Rex Printing Co., Ltd.